COUNTRY EXPLORERS

A Visit to

POLAND

By Charis Mather

BEARPORT
PUBLISHING

Minneapolis, Minnesota

Credits

All images are courtesy of Shutterstock.com, unless otherwise specified. With thanks to Getty Images, Thinkstock Photo, and iStockphoto.

Cover – Michal Ludwiczak, Yasonya. 2–3 – Lukas Bischoff Photograph. 4–5 – GetFocusStudio, Nerthuz. 6–7 – Lukas Bischoff Photograph, T. Lesia. 8–9 – DK-ART, Nahlik. 10–11 – agsaz, Aitor Lamadrid Lopez. 12–13 – Wiola Wiaderek. 14–15 – Teresa Kasprzycka, Wiola Wiaderek. 16–17 – MrMR, Ondrej Prosicky. 18–19 – Magdanatka, vivooo. 20–21 – anmbph, Iwona Fijol. 22–23 – Nowaczyk, seawhisper, tramper79.

Library of Congress Cataloging-in-Publication Data is available at www.loc.gov or upon request from the publisher.

ISBN: 979-8-88509-973-8 (hardcover)
ISBN: 979-8-88822-152-5 (paperback)
ISBN: 979-8-88822-293-5 (ebook)

© 2024 BookLife Publishing
This edition is published by arrangement with BookLife Publishing.

North American adaptations © 2024 Bearport Publishing Company. All rights reserved. No part of this publication may be reproduced in whole or in part, stored in any retrieval system, or transmitted in any form or by any means, electronic, mechanical, photocopying, recording, or otherwise, without written permission from the publisher.

For more information, write to Bearport Publishing, 5357 Penn Avenue South, Minneapolis, MN 55419.

CONTENTS

COUNTRY TO COUNTRY

Which country do you live in?

A country is an area of land marked by **borders**. The people in each country have their own rules and ways of living. They may speak different languages.

Each country around the world has its own interesting things to see and do. Let's take a trip to visit a country and learn more!

Have you ever visited another country?

TODAY'S TRIP IS TO
POLAND!

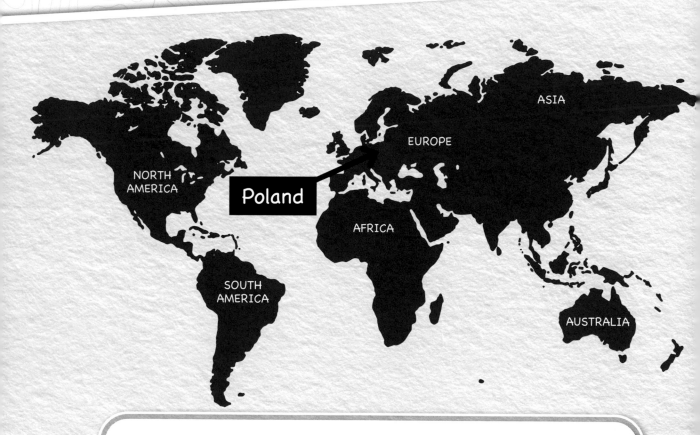

ASIA

EUROPE

NORTH
AMERICA

Poland

AFRICA

SOUTH
AMERICA

AUSTRALIA

Poland is a country in the **continent** of Europe.

FACT FILE

Capital city: Warsaw
Main language: Polish
Currency: Polish zloty
Flag:

Currency is the type of money that is used in a country.

KRAKÓW

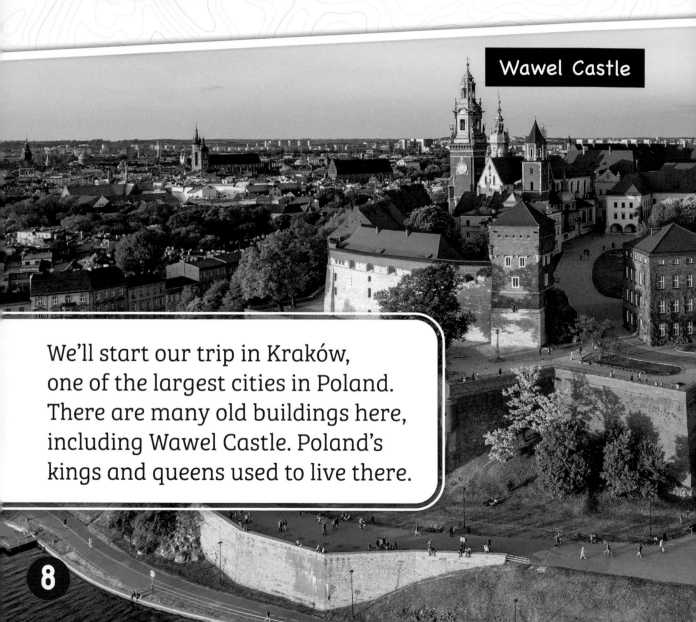

Wawel Castle

We'll start our trip in Kraków, one of the largest cities in Poland. There are many old buildings here, including Wawel Castle. Poland's kings and queens used to live there.

We'll get a great view of the city from the top of Kościuszko Mound. It was built to remember a Polish **general**. The hill is made of soil from different places the general went.

WIELICZKA SALT MINE

Salt art

Next, we'll head underground to the Wieliczka Salt **Mine**. It has about 180 miles (300 km) of **tunnels** and many rooms. There is art made from salt on the walls inside the mine.

One large room in the mine is called St. Kinga's Chapel. All the art was made by hand. Even the **chandeliers** are made of salt!

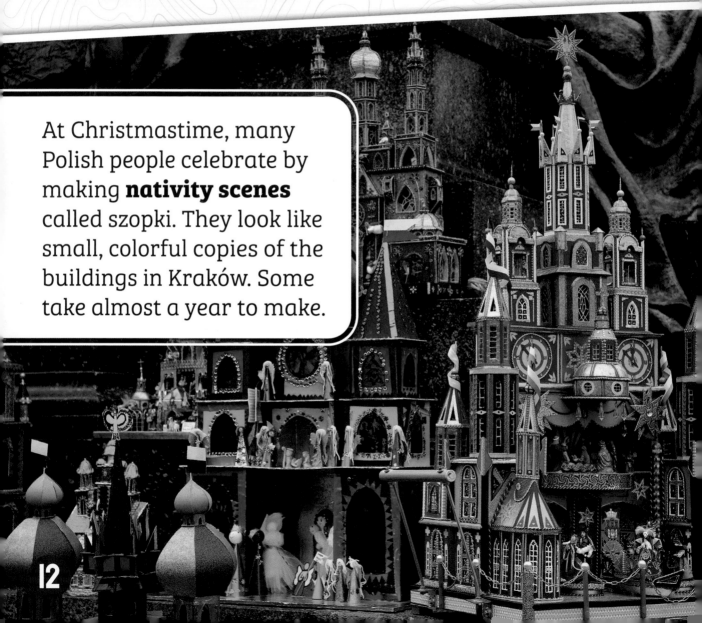

SZOPKI

At Christmastime, many Polish people celebrate by making **nativity scenes** called szopki. They look like small, colorful copies of the buildings in Kraków. Some take almost a year to make.

Many szopki have little **puppets** that are used to tell the story of Christmas. Others have puppets of important people in Poland.

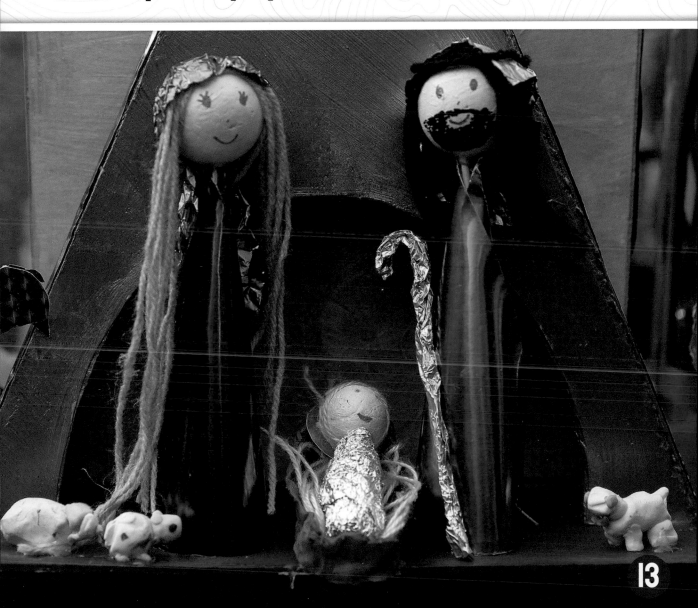

FLOWER CARPETS

Ready to celebrate? Polish people get ready for the holiday of Corpus Christi by making a carpet of flowers. Lots of families help place flowers on the ground in beautiful designs.

Then, people walk along the path. Others gather to watch the group walk past. Sometimes, the flower carpet is almost 3,300 feet (1,000 m) long!

BIAŁOWIEŻA NATIONAL PARK

European bison

Białowieża National Park is a beautiful forest that is full of **wildlife**. It is home to the world's largest group of European bison.

One reason the forest has so much wildlife is because very few people can visit it. Some areas have had almost no people in them for about 800 years.

FOOD

Feeling hungry? First we'll try pierogi. These are a type of dumpling usually filled with meat, cheese, or fruit.

Poppy seed rolls are another popular food in Poland. Flower seeds are crushed up and used as a filling in these cakes. Sometimes, honey is added, too.

Poppy seed rolls are called makowiec (muh-KAU-week).

TREE BEEKEEPING

Today, most **beekeeping** is done in square boxes on the ground. However, some Polish beekeepers use logs instead. The logs are sometimes placed high up in trees.

Beekeepers who use logs think bees should live as **naturally** as possible. When beekeepers collect honey, they usually take only a little. The rest is left for the bees.

BEFORE YOU GO

We can't forget a trip to the Crooked Forest. Here, we will see about 400 trees that grow into strange shapes.

We could also visit some of Poland's amazing wooden churches with tall roofs. Some are hundreds of years old.

What have you learned about Poland on this trip?

23

GLOSSARY

beekeeping looking after bees so their honey can be collected

borders lines that show where one place ends and another begins

chandeliers large, fancy lights that hang from ceilings

continent one of the world's seven large land masses

general an important officer in an army

mine a deep hole or tunnel from which materials are taken

nativity scenes models that show the story of the birth of Jesus Christ

naturally happening in nature without help from people

puppets dolls that can be moved using strings, wires, or your hands

tunnels underground passages

wildlife wild animals living in their natural setting

INDEX